Foreword

All schools in England and Wales now know what is expected of them in the Technology component of the National Curriculum. Currently they are all engaged in planning their responses. How to deliver is the main concern.

The Design and Technology Association has collected in this booklet accounts of the way in which six schools, exhibiting at the National Design and Technology Exhibition at the NEC in October, have tackled the task.

These accounts contain details of planning activities, of projects undertaken and illustrations of their achievements. They provide a context in which visitors to the NEC exhibition will be able to place their impression of what they observed.

Written by teachers for teachers it will allow many schools to benefit from and build upon the experiences described.

Also included in this publication is an article by David Buchan, formerly the secretary of the National Association for Design Education (NADE), a member of DATA's advisory committee. This article entitled 'Design and Technology — Taking a Broad View' is a personal view which has been put to the DATA committee who feel that it will help colleagues engaged in the current debate.

Delivering the Technology Curriculum

The Design and Technology Association
in association with Trentham Books

First published in 1990 by
Trentham Books

Trentham Books Limited
13/14 Trent Trading Park
Botteslow Street
Stoke-on-Trent
Staffordshire ST1 3LY

ISBN: 0 948080 52 3

**British Library Cataloguing in
Publication Data**
Eggleston, John *ed*.
Delivering the Technology Curriculum:
Six case studies in primary and
secondary schools.
1. Education Technology
I. Title
607′

DATA
The Design & Technology Association
Smallpeice House
27 Newbold Terrace East
Leamington Spa
Warwickshire CV32 4ES

Designed and typeset by
Trentham Print Design, Chester and
printed by The Bemrose Press, Chester.

Contents

The search for a topic approach at Severne Junior School, Birmingham

We were invited to exhibit at the NEC. we believe because of good practice developed over a number of years. Now we are working towards developing a realistic approach to the development of DT across the curriculum with children of all ages.

Severne Junior Infant and Nursery school, built sixty years ago in the centre of a large municipal housing estate, has on roll approximately 400 pupils with a 75 place nursery. There are thirteen classes with two parallel classes in most year groups. During 1985 the separate junior and infant schools were combined to form the existing establishment. After the merger a new Headteacher and deputy were appointed.

Initially the merger of the two separate schools provided an ideal opportunity for a whole curriculum audit across all age ranges. It was decided to prioritise and focus the attention of

the entire staff on designated areas: specifically Mathematics, Reading, Science and Writing. The initial curriculum changes were brought about by our professional desire to improve the educational opportunities available at Severne school.

Our curriculum at this time developed through a process of self-evaluation and a lookout for

examples of good practice. Staff were involved in a variety of activities: in-school workshops, visiting speakers and practiners, school exchanges, courses and conferences. An important aspect of our school philosophy is that the curriculum should have a firm base of core subjects, the delivery of which would take account of pupils' interests and staff enthusiasm and expertise.

During the academic year 1985, the school took part in an Information Handling project across the city. This enabled good practice in data handling to be developed with children of varying ages and a recognition of the importance of using IT to support normal curriculum work. We currently had two 480 Z computers and only one disc drive. At this time we were also evaluating our use of constructional material and creative play. We came to the conclusion that while this material was being used for play pur-

poses the design element was not being utilised.

There were two distinct approaches to DT in the classroom: somewhat prescriptive for the junior phase pupils but for the younger children a more creative approach which took account of their interests and needs. We identified a number of reasons for this dichotomy. Firstly, the organisation for the infant phase children was generally more cross-curricular so lent itself more easily to a flexible approach.

Secondly, many of our Junior phase staff still believed that the most important aspect of DT was the final product. Our move towards a process led DT curriculum was certainly influenced by traditional good Infant practice.

In September 1987 we were fortunate to be involved in an ESG science and technology project, which developed work of a technological nature throughout the

school. The emphasis was on developing DT from within a scientific focus. It was still quite an experience to watch the children working constructively and safely with tools and materials that we would not have dreamed of giving them. Very quickly children's and teachers' horizons were

greatly extended. The culmination of our part in this project was an exhibition in the Spring term of 1988. We were all justly proud of our children's achievements. Although the project ran for one term, the benefits in terms of teachers expectations and children's

	Autumn 1990	Spring 1991	Summer 1991
Nursery	Exploring materials/media/process, Travelling to school — Families/Birthdays, All About Me — Celebrations, Me/Friends/Babies, Coming to School — Changes	Wild/Pet/Zoo/Domestic/Farm — Animals — Imaginary/Minibeasts, Care/Habitats/What Eat	Houses, School — Litter/Insects, My Environment — Care, Buildings (Church/Park/Pond/Shops), People — Family/O.A.P. (Visits)
Reception	Making Bags/Tramps, HARVEST HOMES, Natural Resources, Here/There Comparisons, Changes over time, Then/Now comparisons	Materials/Weather/Climate, CLOTHES KITCHEN, Use + function, Use of Pictures + Artefacts, Order, Seasonal Change, Old/New comparison	Rocks, Soil, Water, SPRING BATHROOMS, ANIMAL Adaptations, Order/Sequence, Change over time, New/Young/Old
Y1	Models, Buggies, The Shoe Shop, My Feet — Journeys/Land use/Routes, Shops/Services, The Layout/Plans, Pictures/Artefacts/Before/After, New	Milk, For Clothes, THE POST, Where I Live, Natural Resources, Here/There comparisons, Mapping, Stories of people, When/Where Am I — Family History	EASTER THE POLICE, Soil/Water/Rocks, Jobs/Occupations, Change over time, Photos, Artefacts, Change, Plants Growing etc.
Y2	Use the Garden, 'In the Garden' (Seed Dispersal), CELEBRATIONS, E.G. input Diwali etc, Drop box/Graphics World Study, Transport/ India, Journeys/Ways of travelling, REALITY, Old/New comparisons, Stories/Myths	FABRICS/Dye stuffs (Levers/Forces), Jobs in the House, Natural Resources, ← WEATHER — Natural Forces →, Change over time/Sequence/Order	Minibeast/Animals, SPORTS/GAMES (Sink/Float/Forces), Buildings — Land — Waste/Litter, Use/Size/Function, Improving My Environment, Buildings — Use/ Planning/Mapping, Age/Chronology/Map/Compare/Sort Local Study — Photos
Y3	SD+J > MYSELF Linking Y2/Y3, MY AREA — Design processes, Model of locality, Me / Databases — control Tech, Diagrams/3D, My Surroundings, HAPPY FAMILIES — Look Here, SEASONAL TIME OBJECTS	LAND TRANSPORT (HSU 12), JOURNEYS, A Mouldy Story — Keeping Warm	WEATHER / ANIMAL ADAPTATIONS, HOME MADE TOYS UNINVITED (Minibeasts)
Y4	INVADERS + SETTLERS (HSU 2), Shapes/Materials/Tests — IT procs, HOMES — Area/Settlement/Size, Magnet Games, Windfall — Parachutes (Seed dispersal, Stick together)	SHIPS and SEAFARERS (HSU 8), BRITAIN — Where/What, Land use/Settlement, SPIN A YARN — LOTS OF LIQUID	TUDORS (HSU 3), Services/Shops, A DAY OUT WIRED UP
Y5	VICTORIAN BRITAIN (HSU 4), Machines/Inventions/Problem Solving, European/World study — Land use/Features, TIMBER STORMY WEATHER	SD+HSU: WRITING (changed focus), Features — Contrasts, Weather/Temperature/, Volcanoes/Earthquakes, EARTHY MATTERS — DOLLS HOUSE	EXPLORATION + ENCOUNTERS (HSU 7), WASTE — Care of Environ — ment/Attitudes, CAFE RALLY BOUND
Y6	SYSTEMS/ENVIRONMENTS — Planning, SD LHSU: LOCAL HISTORY, Problem Solving, BIRMINGHAM/Access Green, BIRMINGHAM — Size/Settlement, Data Handling/Graphics/P.E.S.C., FAIR TEST FALLS PARTY	ANCIENT CIVILISATIONS HSU 6, TROPICAL STUDY — including, Environmental issues, HOSPITAL SEASIDE	WATER — Cycle/Rainfall, Rivers etc., PROPAGATING MOVING ON

enthusiasm have remained with us.

These experiences stimulated further developments in DT at Severne, whose policy is that if something is worth doing it is worth doing well! We acknowledge a need for a vast increase in resources. So that we could make informed decisions, we undertook a programme of loaning resource material for evaluation, volunteering for any DT project and providing in-service courses for our staff from local and national sources.

The new Education legislation was met with less trepidation thanks to this preparation and was seen by most of the staff as positive, complementing work we were already doing. With our awareness raised we purchased a variety of equipment: toolboards, flexible commercial construction materials, a science scheme with a built-in technological element and more computers and we moved into the area of computer control.

In our quest for expertise, good practice and general guidance, we visited a number of schools in the city and saw innovative work of a very high standard being developed by committed teachers, often in difficult circumstances. At times we were in awe of what we saw. We soon realised that we could not expect to achieve work of this type or standard in all our classrooms. We made a conscious decision that DT should be an integral part of the curriculum in every class and age group in the school. Our major aim was to ensure that all our children had access to the technological curriculum, that equality of opportunity should not depend upon the strengths or interests of individual teachers. DT claimed its place in our curriculum model and its status soon began to rise. Our successes were documented and experiences shared. For example in July 89 Severne school organised an in-service course on DT for local probationer teachers.

It was time for a policy statement, to formalise the processes we wanted the children to go

through and to ensure continuity and progression. It was decided to await the publication of the National Curriculum orders for guidance and we were pleased to find similar approaches in the document to the process skills we were developing. DT had by now become an integral part of our curriculum planning and we increasingly sought to support topic work through DT. The use of IT as a classroom resource had become second nature to staff and children.

At the start of 1989 we began a process of topic development, examining practice in terms of individual delivery, highlighting the ongoing history and geography through staff workshops. We then planned the year's topics on a year-group basis, alternating the bias towards history and geography. The topics outlined were implemented with regard to National Curriculum English, Maths and Science. We tried to introduce technology through these topics as well as through the Longmans science scheme. We kept asking: why is the technological activity happening? Is it teacher-directed or did the initiative come from the child? The answer to this question may lie in addressing the issues raised in AT1.

We are working towards an emphasis on context, evaluation and planning as indicated in the DT document.

During the summer term of 1990 the draft orders for history and geography enabled us to develop our topic planning further. We adopted a whole school approach in an attempt to foster shared ownership and ensure continuity and progression. Our topic model is based on the spiral curriculum, where broad topics are revisited within the child's primary experience. As far as possible topics are planned not in isolation but as integral parts of various themes which promote the whole curriculum. This approach underpins our curriculum and our philosophy about children's learning, as both our exhibit and our seminar will illustrate.

Developing a structured approach to Design and Technology at Marston Green Junior School, Birmingham

When Marston Green Junior School was chosen to exhibit examples of its work at the NEC, it was taken somewhat by surprise. The school had not yet developed a structured approach to the National Design and Technology Curriculum, nor did it fit the image traditionally associated with schools in the Solihull area — those serving a middle-class population.

But Marston Green was selected for exactly these reasons. Debbie Sheffield, Solihull's Education Inspector explains: "It was clear to me that while a structured approach had not yet fully emerged at the school, design and technology work of real quality was being undertaken. There was obviously enormous enthusiasm and ability amongst the staff for the subjects contributing towards this new curricular area".

Marston Green is a very good example of what can be achieved by a school which does not have the advantages of those situated in more affluent areas.

Built twenty-five years ago to replace the old village school established in 1875, Marston Green Junior School has around 200 pupils aged 7 to 11 roughly half from the nearby Chelmsley Wood Council Estate. There are eight classes, with two parallel classes in each year. Two years ago the school adopted a whole school thematic approach with a 12-term topic plan integrating most aspects of the curriculum.

Some professional staff and curriculum development had already taken place. The Deputy Head had attended LEA in-service courses during the Autumn term of 1989, and the school had used one of its in-service training days in the Spring term to identify design and technology activities as part of its general thematic approach. The final Statutory Orders for design and technology were not yet

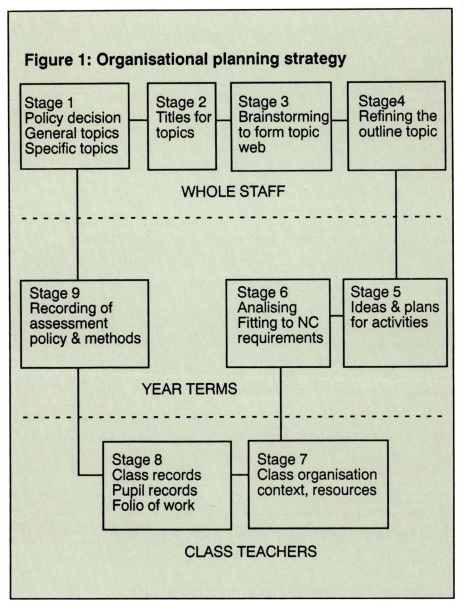

Figure 1: Organisational planning strategy

Stage 1 Policy decision General topics Specific topics	Stage 2 Titles for topics	Stage 3 Brainstorming to form topic web	Stage4 Refining the outline topic

WHOLE STAFF

Stage 9 Recording of assessment policy & methods	Stage 6 Analising Fitting to NC requirements	Stage 5 Ideas & plans for activities

YEAR TERMS

Stage 8 Class records Pupil records Folio of work	Stage 7 Class organisation context, resources

CLASS TEACHERS

published, so draft guidelines were referred to, along with a guidance document produced by the L.E.A.

Using the organisational planning strategy shown in Fig. 1, topic webs were drawn up by each year team. With the confidence and knowledge gained from in-service training, opportunities for the D & T activities were identified.

The second stage included mapping the chosen activities with the four aspects of the programme of study for Key Stage 2 and allied attainment targets. Continuity of planning was ensured by using a planning sheet developed by the LEA and shown in Fig. 2.

An example of a completed sheet appears on page 9.

During the summer term the planned activities were trialled as part of the normal school curriculum, and staff meetings set aside for discussion about their progress.

Some aspects of design and technology were not being covered and would need attention in future planning. Some of the shortfalls identified included:-

Wider media use, especially in clay, food and textile areas;
Greater attention to Attainment Target 1;
The need to develop appropriate methods of recording individual pupil achievement;
A higher profile given to the business context;

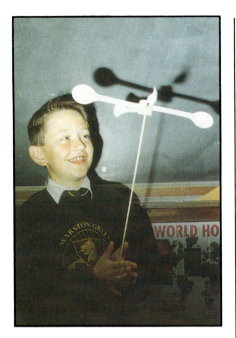

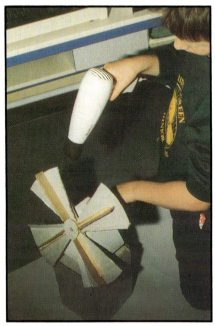

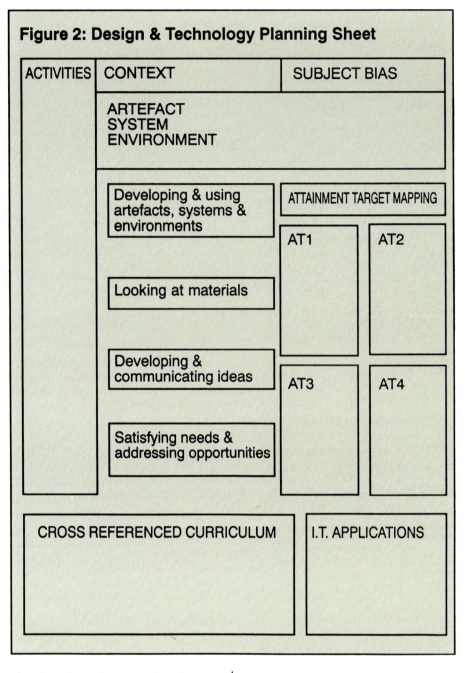

Figure 2: Design & Technology Planning Sheet

ACTIVITIES	CONTEXT		SUBJECT BIAS
	ARTEFACT SYSTEM ENVIRONMENT		
	Developing & using artefacts, systems & environments	ATTAINMENT TARGET MAPPING	
		AT1	AT2
	Looking at materials		
	Developing & communicating ideas	AT3	AT4
	Satisfying needs & addressing opportunities		

CROSS REFERENCED CURRICULUM	I.T. APPLICATIONS

The need for a more balanced approach, extending the scientific route to include more creative and aesthetic elements.

The work displayed at the NEC is the outcome of these summer term trials.

The work of Year 3 children revolved around the theme of *Water.* Two design and technology projects were undertaken,

the first based upon the design and development of an Environmental Studies Area at the school, including a marsh and pond. The local power station at Hams Hall kindly provided help in the form of advice and some plants. Sadly, vandalism was a big problem, but the Year 3 pupils persevered and took a positive approach to the problem by working on ideas to counteract it.

The second project (which children visiting the NEC will have the chance to participate in) involved the design and manufacture of an ice-lolly, and the design of its packaging. The children carried out consumer research in school and at the local shops, so setting it in a business context.

Year 4 children worked on *buildings,* investigating materials builders use, damp-coursing,

Design & Technology Planning Sheet

ACTIVITIES

Stage 1
Short investigations using
lego technic - pulleys, cogs

Safe and proper use of tools

Introduce control software

STAGE 2 Structured design brief
The 'Black Box'
Make an axle turn by turning
another at right angles to it

STAGE 3 Main design projects
Choice from

1. FROM VISIT TO IRONBRIDGE
a) Inclined plane
b) Crane
c) Blowing engine
d) Forge hammer
e) The Ironbridge
d) Coal mine

2. MODERN HISTORY
a) Robot
b) Controlled environment
c) Automatic traffic control
d) Automatic sorting machine

CONTEXT INDUSTRY TOPIC

SUBJECT BIAS Science & CDT

ARTEFACT (s) Series of models

SYSTEM Mechanical systems used in Victorian machinery. Modern electronic systems

ENVIRONMENTS Difference between Industrial revolution conditions & modern factories

Developing and using artefacts, systems and environments

Use video/books to research industrial revolution
Use this info. & knowledge gained thro. lego work to design drive systems
Organise themselves & allocate time within specified timescale.
Test & modify initial drive & control systems

Looking at materials

Instruction in safe use of following - shaper saw, hacksaw, bench hook, drill, glue gun, craft knife, soldering iron, wire stripper.
Select materials from - 8mm timber multiboard, dowel, card, softwood offcuts PVA & hot glue.
Stress limited resource - avoid waste.

Developing and communicating ideas

Provide plans of models showing detail of drive and switching systems.
Keep a record of development and changes made.

Satisfying needs and adressing opportunities

Recognise through modelling the importance of the right working environment and how that environment might be improved.
Recognise the need for safety measures in the work place.

ATTAINMENT TARGET MAPPING

AT1
4c - discuss what it must have been like to work during industrial rev.
4f - Research factors which led to development of iron industry at Ironbridge. Discuss need for pleasant and safe working environment

AT2
4a - Record development of systems from first 2 cog experiment to final model
4b - Development of building in which to house model.
4c - Estimate & plan use of resources before first cut.

AT3
4b - apportion task within group
4e - draw diagrams to modelling

AT4
Review continually the development of models. Possible transcripts of recordings of group discussion. Illustrate to other groups implications of factory environments by use of models.

I.T. APPLICATIONS
4a - Use of DTP package Impression to produce a record of work in the form of a Victorian newspaper.
4b - Use of 'BITS' to control movement and sense environment.
4c - Use of 'Beasty' to control movement.

CROSS REFERENCED CURRICULUM
Science
Attainment targets 10 to 13
- Forces and energy.
AT11 - electricity, 12 - IT
and 6 Materials

Mathematics - measurement and
3D shapes - nets of solids

Language
Reading for information
Industrial revolution booklet
- research & empathy writing

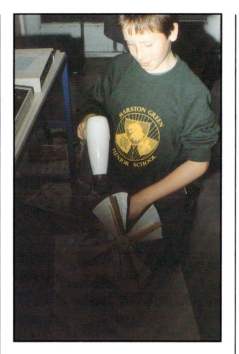
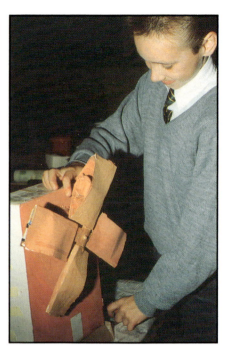

foundations, the bonding and making of bricks and so on. They created structures from the information they had gained and tested them for strength. The resulting models reflected the range of work: some children, studied lighting systems, others roofs; still others demonstrated how joists are designed to carry the weight of additional floors.

Another group looked at gardens and explored the different requirements of different age groups. They were asked to design a garden to suit a specific age group. This also provided an opportunity to use 'The Garden' as an inspiration for textile design.

Feed the World was the topic for Year 5, who considered the problem of raising water for irrigation using wind power. A well was made from a large sweet jar and, using the principles of wheels and cogs, the

pupils designed and built windmills to raise water from it. They also designed a farm to illustrate how all its elements fitted together to create the best possible environment for the farmer.

Year 6 tackled *Industry*, comparing the environments and systems of Victorian times and the modern age. The work was particularly challenging because there was only one term in which to give the children all the skills that, children would in future, progressively acquire throughout Key Stage 2.

The children were thus equipped in three stages. Stage 1 dealt with the necessary knowledge, skills and confidence. Children were taught how to use tools such as hacksaws, drills, glue guns, bench hooks, soldering irons, etc. safely; how to measure accurately so that models designs fitted exactly. Lego Technic was used to demonstrate belt drives, pulleys and cog wheels. The children were also shown how to use computer control software.

Next, they applied knowledge and skills to a structured de-

sign brief. They were given a shoe box with two pieces of dowelling sticking in two of the sides, at right angles to one another and they had to find a means of making one dowel turn when the other was turned.

Stage 3 provided a choice of projects. Half the group studied the Victorian industrial scene and the other half industry today. The first group produced models including a furnace blowing engine, a steam driven forge hammer and a coal mine. The second group's products included a robot which picked up articles, a model factory and an automatic sorting machine.

The children were able to use their computer experience to control lights, motors and sensing devices so imbuing with a degree of realism.

These pilot projects highlighted some problems in this new curriculum area. For one thing it is a high resource area, and resources are in short supply. 'This is particularly true in the primary phase where we are trying to develop a broad and balanced approach,' says John Dainty. 'We have been fortunate in having many parents who have provided the necessary junk materials from home. Schools, however, also need tools, equipment and a variety of hard and soft materials and other commercial resources; building up a stock of these is expensive. One can start with limited resources and junk materials, but by the time children reach Year 6 it is considered essential that they have had opportunities to use and handle the 'real thing.'

Another problem is time. Although design and technology is an exciting curriculum area, it is time consuming. Marston Green's efforts during the term have brought this home to the staff, reinforcing the need to plan and record systematically as a whole school.

There are many positive results, which have emerged from the work Marston Green has undertaken. Staff have found it a valuable awareness creating exercise and it has built up their confidence. Their abilities to recognise design opportunities have been greatly enhanced. The initiatives have revealed the importance of structure and of a progressive approach to the four years of Key Stage 2. "Without it, one cannot expect children to achieve really high quality results', says John Dainty.

Just what Marston Green Junior School has achieved during the activity trial will be apparent to those visiting the exhibition. The staff and children have gained considerable confidence and experience and the school has made tremendous progress in working towards the implementation of National Curriculum design and technology, especially with regard to planning and the organisation and management of resources and the working environment.

Topic work at Courthouse Green Primary School, Coventry

Courthouse Green Primary School was built shortly after the war of a pre-fabricated construction. It is a multicultural school in the over-populated north east of Coventry, in an area where the majority of families were employed at the Morris car factory near the school. This site, derelict for several years, is now being redeveloped, and has a sports centre, a Sainsbury's and Texas superstore and an estate of new houses. The school itself is a large rambling, single storey building, which occupies a huge site, hidden from the main roads by residential housing, which represents a green oasis in a desert of brick and tile. There are few other green spaces around.

Inside the school the accommodation is somewhat inflexible; until ten years ago there were two separate schools, an infant and a junior. It was then amalgamated into a primary school, and in the last few years the numbers have risen steadily so that it now has a role of over four hundred. There are box classrooms, unfortunately without sinks, with the saving grace of wide heated corridors

where the sinks are located, which have bays which can provide additional teaching space. To a visitor, the school has a spacious air, with large entrance areas at either end, two halls, a spacious non- fiction library and the wide corridors; to the teachers, the fifteen smallish box classrooms can be restricting, particularly when they wish to work co-operatively. Outside the school there are three large playgrounds, although they must also accommodate car parking space, and large playing fields and grass to play on, planted generously with all sorts of trees and shrubs. There is also a large area, surrounded by a privet hedge, the garden fences of the surrounding houses and the school's garage. This area used to be kept beautifully as an allotment by one of the school's neighbours: in the eighteen months since his death it has been neglected and has become overgrown. It now presents a golden opportunity for a staff eager to get to grips with technology.

The school is divided into three phases, lower, middle and upper. Lower school represents Key Stage One, with seven classes; in September we will have three Reception classes, with approximately 22 children in each and the help of two education assistants and a full-time Section 11 teacher (Coventry's policy is to admit all rising 5 children in the September of the year in which they will be five, so some of these children will be only just four). There will also be four parallel classes of vertically grouped Y1 and Y2 children, with class sizes of 29 and 30, with the help of a 0.5 Section 11 teacher. Middle and Upper school, representing Key Stage Two, will each have four parallel classes, Middle school with vertically grouped Y3 and Y4 children, and Upper school of Y5 and Y6 children each phase with the help of a 0.5 Section 11 teacher, with class sizes of 29 or 30. Each phase, led by a phase leader, plans together at a weekly meeting; in addition, each member of staff belongs to a National Curriculum working party, which work out aspects of policy for English, Maths and Science and then reports back to the whole staff.

I joined the staff as headteacher in April 1990 from a secondment as advisory teacher for Information Technology in primary schools; this role had led me into providing courses in IT, but also as part of a cross phase team, in writing schemes of work, running courses for teachers of five year olds, planning and delivering seminars on assessment and finally running six two day courses, in a practical workshop format, funded by ESG, on the new Technology orders.

These opportunities have left me fired with enthusiasm for Technology in its widest sense, but coming to terms with the difference between what sounds wonderful at an in-service training course and the reality of its implementation in the school and classroom. As a staff we have to wrestle with the introduction of Technology across both Key Stages and simultaneously designing schemes of work for the next two years and coming to grips with teacher assessment, recording and reporting.

Our planning for Technology began rather late, due to the late appearance of the orders and the even later delivery of the non-statutory guidance. We set aside after school sessions for the whole staff to become familiar with the document and to work together on technology tasks so that we could come to some shared understanding of what

we meant by technology. These sessions were enormously enjoyable, but inevitably raised problems and unanswered questions. We instituted a technology audit — a review of what technological activities we already engaged in, the resources we already had, what we felt we still needed and where we could store it so that it would be accessible to the children when they needed it.

Like most schools, we can provide experiences for children in graphic media, although we don't yet have cameras; textiles is an area where we need to plan carefully for children to dye, print, weave, knit and sew, design and create garments. We have materials for construction, kits, junk modelling, wood, clay, sand and water, but are quite sure we don't have enough, and are unsure how a limited budget will cope with constantly replenishing consumable materials. We do have newly purchased tools and two donated work benches and one of our own, so can provide at least enough tools to share between each phase. To provide experience with food, we have a Baby Belling which is not mobile and at the other end of school from the KS1 children. There is also a microwave, admittedly on a trolley, but not easy to negotiate up the flight of steps which separates the old infant and junior school.

Stairs are also a problem with our computer trolleys. Our aim is to provide a complete computer system for each classroom. So far

we have achieved a system shared between two classes — better than some schools but still not adequate to meet the demands of the Information Technology Capability profile component. We have enough money to make sure that each system has its own trolley and printer, but for a school of over 400 pupils we could make constant use of a colour printer, not as a luxury but as an essential part of children's design experience, and will have to try to raise funds for one. The largest demand of Information Technology is in time for the staff to receive hands-on training. We can provide a certain amount in school using LEATGS time, and the staff are very keen to take machines home at weekends and holidays, particularly to come to grips with the new Archimedes computers, but training for a large staff will take time, and we will have to rely on each other's expertise.

We have decided to create a Technology bay in each of our three corridors, to be accessible to all the children and to store resources centrally, except the potentially dangerous or the highly desirable and portable! Each bay will have a workbench and we will be able to store paper, card, junk modelling materials, wood, fabric, paint and glues. Opportunities for co-operative teaching arise, since groups of children from different classes will be able to share the workspace.

As primary teachers, we believe, we have considerable, and probably undervalued, skills as designers — we arrange the furniture in our classrooms to maximise the children's learning opportunities, we organise the day according to their needs, we put up displays, write worksheets and workcards, provide space to store coats, lunchboxes, workbooks; we design imaginative play corners for children — homes, cafes, hairdressers, hospitals, stations, shops, castles — and design each lesson carefully to match the needs and abilities of each child in our care. Primary children, if they are lucky, spend their time in a stimulating and visually appealing environment. They bring with them their experiences of the world, where they are surrounded by technology, not only their proficiency with video recorders and computers, but also their familiarity with beautifully produced picture books, amazing graphics heralding television programmes, the ease of ordering a meal at Macdonalds or having the cost of their groceries added by a bar code reader at the supermarket. They are aware of traffic systems, bicycles, the way playgrounds are laid out, the need for litter to be efficiently collected. To teach Technology to the children at Courthouse Green, then, we should exploit our own experiences and environment. The school itself, both inside and out, is rich with opportunity, from evaluating pop-up books or the way the mid-morning milk is distributed designing a wildlife garden or making signs to ensure that visitors are made to feel welcome and don't get lost.

Beyond the gates we have traffic, roads, several small parades of shops, sports centre and large superstores, a variety of housing spanning several centuries, a play area and, within walking distance, an entire shopping centre. There are several small factories, a large police station, churches, two mosques and a temple we can walk to; we are certainly not short of contexts for our work. The technology document, moreover, encourages us to believe that the technology tasks the children undertake should be holistic. We are not trying to teach individual skills with hacksaws or paint but ensuring that the children receive the tuition they need to accomplish the task they have undertaken. We do not wish to pick off each Attainment Target in turn but to ensure that through any given task — planning a teddy bears' picnic, designing a poster to advertise the Leavers' disco, making a model of the new carpark — the children have the opportunity to assess need for, plan, make and evaluate their finished work, and then perhaps start again.

In terms of our planning for technology at Key Stage One, the tasks the children will undertake will evolve from the topic work which is ongoing in their classroom. The key concept to be developed in the Autumn term in Conservation, and the children's learning opportunities in English, Maths and Science will largely be derived from a topic based on making a wildlife garden on the overgrown allotment. Technology offers us a vehicle for avoiding the curriculum overload that threatens learners in

Key Stage One in particular, and a way of delivering the other subjects with coherence and relevance to the children. The most difficult part for the teachers to deal with, in the planning process, is the necessity to take a step back and allow the children to identify needs and opportunities and suggest their own solutions. In making a wildlife garden we may expect that the children will want to visit other gardens, photograph, paint, model and talk about what they have seen. They might visit the garden centre near school, and begin to estimate the price of things they require. They will need to design different parts of the garden, consider a pond, assess the suitability of the present fencing, decide on the right kind of gate, write to potential sponsors and local wildlife groups. They will need adult help to dig and plant, consider an opening ceremony and an appropriate guest list, write invitations, provide refreshments and entertainment for their guests and record the event in many different ways. What the teachers won't be able to predict is which children, or groups or whole classes will adopt different parts of the work — if we direct the children too much, they won't have been learning Technology.

What we have to do now is gather our resources, mental and physical, and see where the children take us; where can we get four very cheap, polaroid cameras, with even cheaper film?

Christine Lockwood
Headteacher

Planning a holistic approach at Brinsworth Comprehensive School, Rotherham, South Yorkshire

Brinsworth Comprehensive School is an 11-18 mixed comprehensive school which serves the Brinsworth, Whiston, Catcliffe and Canklow areas of Rotherham. Currently there are 1,260 pupils on roll, including a Sixth Form of 200. The school is housed in modern, well-equipped buildings and has excellent facilities, the Design and Technology area being no exception. In an ideal world, Design and Technology should be in a suite of rooms in one building, so that pupils have ready access to the specialists facilities. In a less than ideal world, the Design and Technology facilities in Brinsworth are well placed and well resourced.

■ Background Information

The Craft, Design and Technology and Home Economics departments have always been

progressive in outlook, the staff eager to provide an interesting and appropriate curriculum for their pupils. Teaching strategies include investigative and experimental approaches and both departments use a design process to enable pupils to work with a range of materials. The departments have always encouraged pupils to attain high standards, which is reflected in the examination results.

In January 1989, the school was invited to become involved in a pilot scheme for Design and Technology being developed by the National Design and Technology Education Foundation. Mr W H Cavill, the Senior Adviser for Rotherham, provided documents as a basis for our discussions about the implications of the invitation. Having studied these documents, the Heads of Departments of CDT, Business Studies, HE and IT all agreed to be involved with the pilot scheme, seeing it as an opportunity to plan, prepare and evaluate Design and Technology activities whilst at the same time

allowing staff to consider the different teaching strategies which might be necessary.

■ Implementing Design and Technology

Design and Technology is one of the most exciting, provocative and demanding initiatives to emerge from the National Curriculum. Involvement with the pilot scheme has provided us with an In-Service programme which has enabled us to develop an understanding of the philosophy of DT, the holistic approach, learning strategies, monitoring and tracking, assessment procedures and assessment and the importance of staff team development.

Hence our priorities this year were to develop a holistic approach to the curriculum through an organisation appropriate to the needs of both pupils and staff.

■ Organisation procedures

1. First Year 1989/90. Number of Pupils: 228.

2. Numbers of Tutor Groups: 6 for each half-year group.

3. Staffing: (a) A total of ten members of staff, viz:

   Home economics: 4

   Craft, Design and Technology: 4

   Business Studies: 2

Note: Art timetabled separately but taught in close conjunction with the DT team. Members of the DT team also taught Information Technology.

(b) Seven members of staff were allocated to each half-year group. i.e. 6 tutors plus one member of staff to supply support.

(3 HE, 3 CDT, 1 BS)

4. Timetable allocation: 3 periods per half-year group per week.

5. SEN provision: parental support and Sixth Form support was available to each team for individual pupils or groups of pupils with specific learning needs.

Within this framework, the following principles were applied:-

(a) Each pupil was allocated to a tutor group (grouping being on a mixed ability basis on the recommendation of the first year tutor and SEN department).

(b) Each tutor group was allocated:

— a home base

— colour coding for recognition/identification purposes.

(c) Each pupil received:-

— a 'Design and Technology' folder to be retained in the home base;

— a 'Design and Technology' plastic wallet for current work;

— a pupil record card (colour coded);

— an assessment/monitoring card;

— a colour coded 'Design and Technology' badge;

— a series of self-help task sheets/work sheets.

(d) Tutor groups and bases were fixed for the year, but working groups within the tutor group changed every unit.

■ Developing a holistic approach

In developing our scheme of work for this National Curriculum subject we were concerned to establish staff confidence and security. We were also conscious of the needs of Year One pupils for stability and security when first transferring from the Junior School.

Initial planning centred around existing syllabuses for Year One HE and CDT in order to identify possible cross-curricular themes. Brainstorming produced the idea of developing a foundation unit which was given the simple but important title Design and Technology in Brinsworth Comprehensive School. We wanted pupils to have some structured learning experience to familiarise themselves with safe working practices with a range of equipment and materials and at the same time to acquire a knowledge base for research and development of the design process.

The first unit also introduced the design process through the idea of designing a course logo. The 'Design and Technology Badge' incorporates a logo design and the pupil's name, becoming the pupil's 'passport' to movement round the DT area.

Subsequent units have evolved from brainstorming ideas to identify an appropriate context which can be cross-referenced to the Programmes of Study, Objectives identified and appropriate resources prepared. Each unit is introduced to a half year group in a stimulus session which may involve displays, video, role play and questionnaires. Pupils then discuss the issues in small groups within the tutor group, to identify possible outcomes and then select the area in which they will work. The development of each unit has involved all pupils experiencing short pupil-centred learning tasks so as to give breadth to their knowledge and learning experiences. Pupils are expected to 'make' rather than model artefacts and record their activity in a design folder.

We went on to establish three further topics entitled: 'It's Rubbish', addressing pollution; 'Let's contain it', concerned with artefacts

and systems for organisation; and finally 'Fairground Activity Day'. This last has undoubtedly been the most successful in terms of developing the cross-curricular themes and in particular the issues of economic awareness. Pupils were highly motivated and produced appropriate artefacts, systems and environments while enjoying their learning experience. A video was made of the event and examples of the pupils' work will be on exhibition at the National Exhibition Centre.

■ Future Developments

At the end of an exciting and exhausting year, the team have carried out an in-depth evaluation of the course to shape plans for the future. A scheme of work

describes the aims, objectives, course content, resources, cross-references to the programmes of study and assessment procedures. The major outcome of evaluation has been concern about insufficient time to develop units so the initial course has been modified by removing one of the units. Each has been further developed by improving content and resources. The course has maintained its balance of structure and open-ended tasks and will provide pupils with a range of learning experiences.

DT is challenging and must be seen as a positive way of crossing cross-curricular boundaries. It is also an avenue for real equality of opportunity.

We have, naturally, encountered problems but resolving them, has led to significant steps in course development and in staff development. Success can be measured in a variety of ways:-

the development of an organisation structure which allows pupils access to a full range of specialist facilities on a 'needs driven basis' without disrupting or inconveniencing the rest of the school.

More significantly, success can be measured in the achievements of our pupils — they are more creative and confident and undoubtedly gain much satisfaction from their DT work.

The success of this course must be attributed to the commitment of the staff and the support received from our Headteacher, Mr M Gray, the Senior Management of the school and the Authority's School Liaison Adviser, Mr T Slack.

Christine Stoor
Coordinator for Design Technology.

Design and Technology in the whole curriculum at St Benedict's Upper School, Suffolk

■ The County

Suffolk Education Committee has a policy known as 'The Suffolk Curriculum', which contains the best elements of lively and imaginative curricula with many of the elements of national curriculum. The Suffolk Curriculum emphasises methods of teaching and learning and the needs of each student. It supports cross-curricular experiences with subjects and the acquisition of the skills, knowledge, attitudes and values that build students' confidence to play an active and purposeful part in society. Suffolk has for many years been in the forefront of curricular development, including Co-ordinated Science, Records of Achievement, Appraisal and, more recently, Co-ordinated Science/CDT/HE.

■ The School

Situated in Bury St Edmunds, St Benedict's is the Catholic Upper School for the western area of

HE1 Above: Yr 9. Energy investigations. Measuring electricity consumption and cost effiveness of appliances using the energy educator.

Suffolk and parts of Cambridgeshire and Norfolk. The catchment area is therefore very large with

the majority of students travelling to school by bus.

The school occupies an attractive site of six acres on the northern outskirts of Bury, a large historic market town about 30 miles east of Cambridge. It was opened in January 1967 as a Secondary Modern School and in 1971 the school was added to and re-organised as a 13-18 Comprehensive Upper School which now has a fully delegated budget.

Currently the school has a Headteacher plus 27 teachers and a student roll of approximately 400, with a Sixth Form of 100. Since September 1986, the Sixth Form operates jointly with the Sixth Form of neighbouring County Upper School. This allows students to choose from an extensive range of 'A' level courses and a one year CPVE course with various GCSEs. The combined Sixth Form amounts to approximately 220.

The school's relatively small size and its church foundation enables it to provide a relaxed, caring but purposeful atmosphere whilst maintaining high academic standards. The emphasis is on school-based rather than departmental resources and the level of staff co-operation is high. The library, AVA centre and computer resource area are all available to the students, who are encouraged to identify and use the resources they need.

■ The Whole Curriculum

Pastoral care and guidance are given a high priority throughout the school including the Sixth Form. However, the size of the school combined with a need to maintain RE in the core does re-

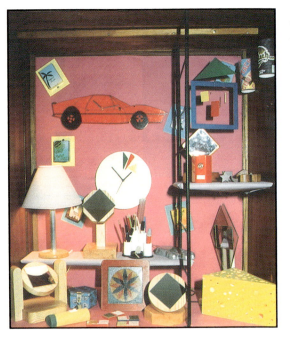

CDT1 Above: Illuminated display of CDT products

HE2 Below U6th Social Evening Prep. After A-levels upper sixth preparing for their social evening

strict room for manoeuvre in curriculum planning. It does, at least, serve to concentrate the mind on what is essential.

The school was part of Suffolk's first phase of TVEI extension in September 1988. This enabled us to resource developments which had been planned in the school for some time. The curriculum model overleaf summarises the position we plan to be in by September 1991. Co-ordinated Suffolk Science, CDT and Home Economics was part of the school's TVEI submission in 1988. Suffolk Science was introduced in September 1988. The first year of the Home Economics and CDT 3 year GCSE course begins in September 1990.

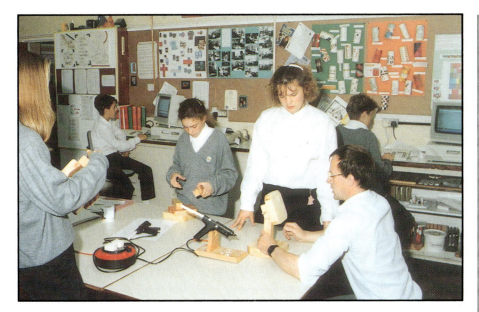

Investment in hardware and in-service training for information technology has been consider-able. Although a computer re-source room has been retained for group work, emphasis has been on the utilisation of termi-nals throughout the school, monitoring their use against the entitlement for all students in IT across the curriculum.

The second foreign language is taught by withdrawal to create a compulsory 'aesthetic' option block with its own injection of hardware. In this way, all stu-dents follow an aesthetic course which also contributes to the technology entitlement through work on CAD, art and musical composition work using MIDI. Most departments are now mak-ing a contribution towards teach-ing different aspects of IT.

■ Liaison

Liaison with our middle school takes place at subject level, with shared INSET for National Cur-riculum. Exchange teaching be-tween schools has also been planned, so that content and pro-cesses are familiar and consistent throughout key stage 3.

■ The Co-ordinated Development

The Co-ordination of Science, CDT and Home Economics is part of Suffolk's response to TVEI and National Curriculum. The co-ordinated course has been de-signed for students of all abilities. It consists of three separate Mode 3 GCSE courses: Co-ordinated Science, CDT Design and Tech-nology and Home Economics. All have been approved by SEAC. Each course consists of compul-sory units of work, some com-

CURRICULUM MODEL SEPTEMBER 1991											
	GUID	RE	PE	Eng	Maths	Co-ord Sci	Hums	Fr	Co-ord CDT/HE	Aesth Art Mu	Ger
Yr 9	1	2	2(1)	4	4	5(4)	3	3(2)	3	2 1	(3)
Yr 10	1	2	2	4	4	5	3	3	3(2)	Art, Mu or Phot 3(2)	(2)
Yr 11	1	2	2	4(3)	4(3)	5	3(2)	3	CDT or HE 3	Art, Mu or Phot 3	(3)

Notes
i) Based on a 30 x 50 minute week.
ii) German is by withdrawal — periods in brackets apply.
iii) An additional 20 minutes Tutor/Assembly time each morning.
iv) Careers, Health Education, Information Technology, Economic and industrial Understanding are delivered across the curriculum and by special events.
v) An ROA programme has been running for some years.

HE3 Left: Yr 9 Analysing diet and energy consumption from food diaries.

port and an AVA/Resource Technician.

It was envisaged that the Co-ordinated course would provide a core entitlement for all pupils, address sex stereotyping and achieve a better balance for the previously traditional subject areas. Co-ordination of subjects allows for collaboration between teachers in developing resource materials, eliminates overlap and addresses cross-curricular issues. It also allows for greater flexibility with timetabling since some units of work may be transferred quite easily from one subject area to another (eg Science and Home Economics) and a number of units are shared between areas.

mon to two of the courses. All three courses have common teaching/learning strategies, continuous assessment, co-ordination of content with a process-based approach and consistent with technology in the National Curriculum. Staff at St Benedict's have been actively involved with writing and trialling materials during the development of these courses.

The full-time equivalent staffing for Science, CDT, HE is at present 4.5, 1.5 and 1.0 respectively, with technical support of 1.5, 0.5 and 0.5. There is also an additional 0.5 cross-curricular technical sup-

■ Facilities

TVEI funding, together with advisory teacher support and much hard work by the teaching staff and technicians, have transformed technology at St Benedict's.

CDT now has two multipurpose rooms. One room has a greater emphasis on design and production and the other on design and graphics. Both are clean, bright, stimulating and appropriate for designing and making. The Home Economics room is now also multipurpose, areas having

CDT3 Left: Yr 9 Applying first coat of varnish to mirrors

been created for various aspects of the course.

The environment our students work in has been given high priority. The selective use of lighting, music, colour and dis-

HE4 Above: Yr 9 Equipment comparison using knives, peelers and food processor.

CDT4 Below: Yr 9 Packaging — graphics work plus items of GCSE course work

plays are all designed to stimulate learning and creativity. The role the students play in displaying their work in the teaching areas is a valuable part of their technological experience.

The CDT accommodation originally consisted of a Metalwork/Motor Vehicle workshop and a Woodwork/Plastics room. Over the years these had accumulated the smells, grease and unattractive appearance traditionally associated with such areas.

The Home Economics room, although always light and clean, was basically a cooking area. Textiles had to be done in a nearby classroom.

The students' identification of needs and opportunities, the pro-

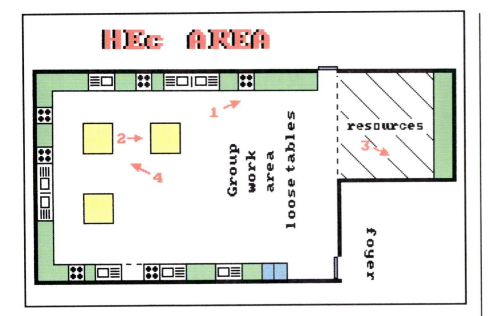

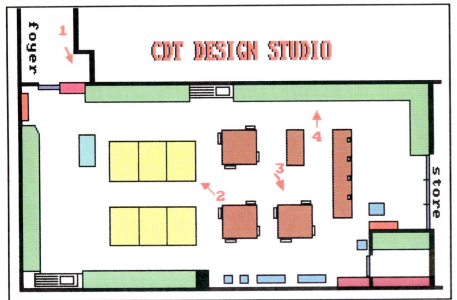

duction of design specifications, the generation of designs, and the realisation and evaluation of their designs have generated the need for areas arranged and equipped to support a wide range of design and technological activities. Students also make full use of whole school resources.

■ The Future

Issues still to be addressed include the detailed planning of schemes of work for national curriculum courses, particularly key stage 3 with our feeder middle school; and the development of assessment models which will enable us to build a record of achievement for the students as they complete Key stage 3 and progress through Key stage 4. Work on monitoring and accrediting achievement in information technology is already under

way; discussions for the closer involvement of Art are still in their infancy. The size of the school has made it impossible to maintain business studies on the curriculum and delivery of these aspects of the entitlement requires more attention than it has been possible to give so far.

The Technology, Research, Information, Problem Solving Course (T.R.I.P.S.) at Greenhead Grammar School, West Yorkshire

Greenhead Grammar School, Keighley, West Yorkshire, is a 13-18 mixed comprehensive school of about 1,000 students. The children progress to Greenhead through a middle school system in the areas to the north and east of Keighley town centre.

Design Technology is housed in nine purpose-built rooms of various vintages. Information Technology is accommodated in three rooms. All twelve rooms have been refurbished within school using a self-help approach and a small financial contribution from TVEI. Our teaching of technology needed developing so that it was no longer seen as a separate entity, but rather as an integral part of our curriculum. The Technology Research Information Problem Solving T.R.I.P.S course commenced four years ago and is still developing to facilitate the pro-

Above: Word Processing results of a survey.

cess of students' acquisition of technological competencies.

■ T.R.I.P.S.
A Cross-Curricular Technology Course

This new and exciting course for students at Key Stage 3, is designed to approach Technology

in a new way, cutting across curriculum boundaries. It is based on Electronics, Design Technology, Information Technology, Food and Fabric Technology and Media Technology, and aims to show that Technology is not a subject with a particular content but rather a process which develops skills throughout the whole curriculum. The T.R.I.P.S. course aims to provide students with skills to approach problems through investigation and research, to acquire knowledge to solve relevant and real technological problems, to foster initiative and resourcefulness, to be technologically aware, to be able to co-operate and accept responsibility in a group situation, to improve communication skills and to be able to make judgements which are aesthetically, technically, economically and morally sound.

Left: Students researching for electronic items and costing.

The course has two elements:

(1) An introduction; to raise awareness of the scope and range of opportunities in each of the five contributory areas.

(2) A Small Business Scheme:- the major element of the course, divided into three phases each containing different tasks in each phase. (See Fig. 1) Tasks may be directed at internal company management or towards the current project and allow pupils to tackle problems encountered by a small business in the market place. Groups of pupils are responsible for developing various aspects of the company and are expected to produce and present finished project work in a set format including, where appropriate, a finished piece of technological hardware. Pupils are assessed on a regular basis, both by verbal appraisal and by a written personal Record of Achievement. (See Figs. 2a & b).

A typical scenario for the T.R.I.P.S. Small Business Scheme would be a small design company, The Design House (Fig. 3) which has been developing over the last two years and has now been asked to advise on the production of a total working package and corporate image to suit a client's needs. The company has been called in to advise a national

Figure 1

T . R . I . P . S Small Business Scheme.

Small Business Scheme stage/work matrix.

PHASE		Business Tech	Media Tech	Electronic Tech	Design Tech	Food & Material Tech
1		Personnel database	Petrol Promotion	Security System	Company name & logo	Packed Lunches
1		Company payroll	Newspaper Advert	Warning Device	Planning of site	Ergonomics
2		Ergonomics databook	Menu cards	Electronic Sign	Company transport	Company Uniform
2		Product costings	ID cards	Cash/ EFTPOS Terminal	Planning the building	Protective clothing
3		Employing staff	TV/radio advert & jingle	Intercom System	Eating unit	Interior design
3		Promotional booklet	Promotional gifts	Keeping Hot/Cool	Playground	Presentation Buffet

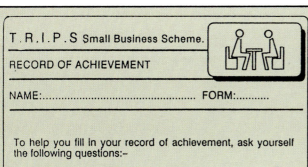

T.R.I.P.S Small Business Scheme.

RECORD OF ACHIEVEMENT

NAME:..................................... FORM:...........

To help you fill in your record of achievement, ask yourself the following questions:-

1. How well have I worked with my partner?

2. Did I lead the work, was it shared or did I follow or copy the work of others?

3. How did I use my time, was I organised or did I waste it?

4. What do I think of the group's work, is it finished, how could I have made it better?

5. Did I understand the work fully, just some of it, or none of it?

6. Did I do any of the work at home, eg getting information or collecting leaflets to help me or my group?

7. What have I enjoyed doing most and why?

8. What did I do best?

9. What can I improve so that it is better next time?

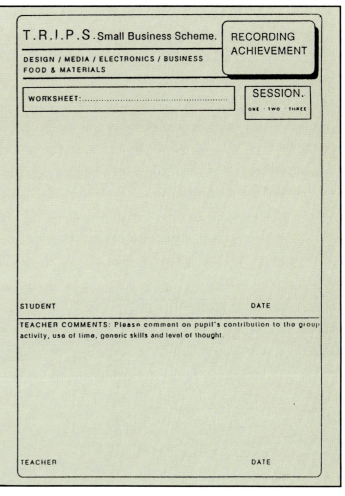

T.R.I.P.S. Small Business Scheme.

DESIGN / MEDIA / ELECTRONICS / BUSINESS FOOD & MATERIALS

RECORDING ACHIEVEMENT

WORKSHEET:.....................................

SESSION.
ONE · TWO · THREE

STUDENT   DATE

TEACHER COMMENTS: Please comment on pupil's contribution to the group activity, use of time, generic skills and level of thought.

TEACHER   DATE

Figure 2a

Left: Making electronic sign.

catering company with outlets in motorway service stations, which needs to remain competitive and retain its high profile in the market place. The Design House has been contracted to produce a complete design package encompassing company name, logo, transport and uniform, interior design, furniture design, promotional materials, provision of children's play area, communication and security.

The structure has proved to be crucial to the perceived success of the scheme. In a typical year group (and at present we teach T.R.I.P.S. only in Year 9, due to

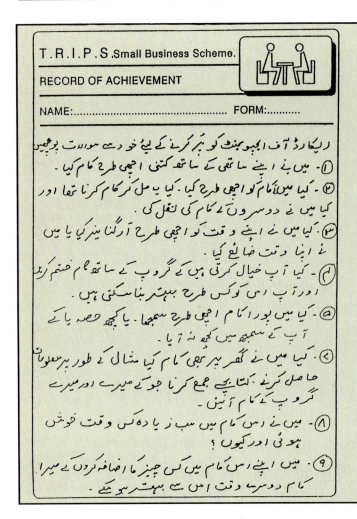
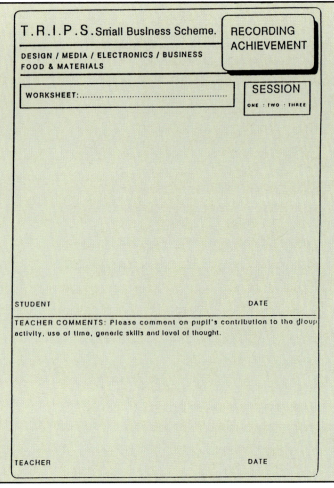

Figure 2b

pressure to teach to an examination in Years 10 and 11), there would be ten registration forms. Each of these would have 20-22 children of mixed ability, race and gender. The T.R.I.P.S. scheme would be delivered to half the year group at a time (five form groups). Each of these forms would be randomly allocated to a Design and Technology teacher. There is an additional teacher, who provides support for students where necessary. The teacher and form would work together to form a 'company'. The company's first task would be to decide the responsibilities each student would undertake within each area of the company and who would take on the role of manager in each of the small groups of students (4 or 5) going to each area. The managers' main tasks are to organise the work in each area (Electronics, Design Technology, Information Technology, Food and Fabric Technology and Media Technology) to meet the demands of the company and to report back to the management meeting on progress and future targets at the first lesson each week. T.R.I.P.S. is allocated 2 x 50 minute periods per week in a 30 period week.

■ **Practical Application**

It is important to understand that T.R.I.P.S. is a small business simulation; not a mini-enterprise scheme. The major difference is that students are involved in a much larger range of problems and situations, that a small company is likely to face in the market place. We have attempted to make the company, its operation and the work it is involved in, as realistic as possible within a school situation. There are some aspects of T.R.I.P.S. which are not found in any other course.

Each of the 10 companies (forms) in the year group work as the small design company, The Design House, (Fig. 3) using the same brief but, in the manner of all children, reacting to it and producing results in very different ways. The tasks are fully resourced and have an accompanying worksheet designed as a

Right: Cutting out card patters for waiter/ess head gear.

guide to enable all students to achieve success in each one.

The thirty activities are organised into three phases so that a natural progression of work and information can flow through the scheme. Some tasks need to be done first, since others depend on them. The structuring of the work has allowed a number of study paths to be developed within the tasks, so that students can follow a theme throughout the scheme. For example, students who have worked on the Ergonomics task in Food and Materials Technology may follow this through into Ergonomics databook (Business Technology Phase 2) and then into Children's Playground (Design Technology Phase 3) (See Fig. 1). Students are allowed to follow a study path or make a company choice about where they will move at the end of each phase.

The three phases are treated as separate stages, so that we can achieve a number of tasks. Firstly, it allows all students to experience three of the five areas, which may be choices based on personal interests or company-directed as a result of the management meetings. Secondly, it allows a presentation and evaluation session for each company at the end of each phase, in order that current progress and work can be reviewed and enables Recording of Achievements to occur. At the end of the whole scheme each

T.R.I.P.S
TECHNOLOGY, RESOURCES, INFORMATION AND PROBLEM SOLVING
DESIGN HOUSE
BACKGROUND

The company is a small firm formed 5 years ago by two colleagues. They initially did small contract design work, producing such items as advertising materials, company logos, handbooks etc. The company has developed during the last two years in a number of areas due to demand. They needed to be able to produce a total design package which covers a wide range of extra areas, such as ideas for fast food, retail outlet design, stationery, packaging work, clothing and uniform. The demand continues to be for one of total working package and corporate image to suit a company's need.

The firm has just brought in people who are experts in video and computer graphics. A studio has been set up and they are now able to produce advertising/display materials using their two new Hi-tec tools.

The firm now has experts in the areas of:

Electronics, Graphic Design, the Media, Food preparation and presentation, Business organisation and Fabrics.

SITUATION

A national food company with outlets involved in motorway service stations needs to remain competitive in this ever increasing market.

The Design House has been asked to look at the following areas:

- Company name and logo
- Company transport and livery
- Exterior layout of a sample site
- Company uniform and protective clothing
- The interior design
- Provision of a play area for children
- Furniture design
- Promotional booket
- Expansion plans
- Signage
- Communication on site
- Security
- Menu cards
- Promotion in the media

FIGURE 3

Left: Drawing up the final proposal for the transport

student will have three Record of Achievement profiles, one for each area they have worked in. Finally, each company gives a presentation involving the display of students' work and a verbal explanation of their design proposals to all the other companies.

There is still much to do, but we feel we have a structure that will take us through and meet National Curriculum requirements at Key Stage 3. The T.R.I.P.S. course has injected new life into the department. It has provided remarkable motivation for our students. Our discipline problems are minimal and low achievers have found a medium through which they can shine amongst their peers and form bands of trust. However, the demands on teachers are greater than ever, as we are now not only educators but have also to take on roles as managers and facilitators.

Photocopiable Teaching Packs are available for this course at a cost of £21.50 (cheques payable to T.R.I.P.S.) from Brian Smith, 15 Willow Tree Close, Longlee, Keighley, West Yorkshire BD21 4RZ. Tel: 0535 664819.

Above: Drawing up the grid for positioning Logo on transport.

The Aims of DATA

DATA was established in November 1989, with funding from the Smallpeice Trust, to:

☐ represent the newly defined curriculum area called Design and Technology

☐ to give it the recognition and esteem which it deserved.

It aims to:

☐ support teachers and all those concerned with delivery of this cross-curriculum experience

☐ produce teacher support and pupil resource material

☐ run courses, conferences, workshops

☐ provide a forum for discussion for those charged with delivery of the National Curriculum proposals for Design and Technology, and

☐ represent effectively, in discussion with Central Government, training agencies, other subject associations, the interests of Design and Technology.

The Smallpeice Trust was established in 1966, 'to improve manufacture by Design'. It has, since that date, run courses for design engineers and others employed in the manufacturing industry. More recently, recognising the importance of an involvement at an earlier stage, it has run residential problem- solving courses for selected pupils aged 14-19, employing natural communicators like Professor Heinz Wolfe and others. These have been highly successful.

In 1989 a proposal was made to the Smallpeice Board that it should establish a professional association, similar to ASE (Association for Science Education) to represent the new curriculum area.

Having commissioned one of its Fellows to Produce a feasibility study, and having consulted all subject associations involved in this newly defined area and elicited their support, at a conference held in the Royal Society of Arts, it funded the launch of DATA, which over the last eight months has been enormously successful.

DATA already boasts a membership of well over 1000 and this will significantly increase once we have engaged in a planned publicity campaign. We have, for example, whole LEAs who have requested that we enrol all their schools.

We have staged, at Central Government's request, a seminar to discuss the draft Order for Technology. This allowed us, within the week, to present the Secretary of State with a transcript of the proceedings (a transcript requested by the CBI, The Fellowship of Engineering and other employment agencies). This influenced the redrafting and led to a stiffening of the proposals and re-established the importance of 'practical outcomes'.

We ran a major conference for 450 delegates (another 150 were turned away) at which the Secretary of State made his first public utterances on the way ahead with Technology.

We have produced a termly journal, an international research and curriculum journal, occasional publications on issues which are topical. eg. an issue available at the NEC exhibition which describes the approaches of the six schools which are featured in the exhibition.

We have already engaged in major research and curriculum development projects, eg. with funding from EITB and support from Bradford LEA, we have released teachers from first, middle and secondary schools to produce teacher support material which, after trialling, will be widely disseminated on the DAT network.

DATA in its development:

☐ has absorbed EIDCT, CODATA and CLCDT

☐ NADE and ISCDTA have taken executive decisions to join and await now their AGMs to ratify these decisions

☐ DESTECH has approached us to seek collaboration with a view to eventual merger. NATHE seeks affiliation

☐ it is in the process of establishing a regional network and local activity/support groups

☐ a number of training institutions are seeking to establish DATA nodes.

DATA has the benefit of a strong advisory group, drawn nationally and representing those disciplines which feature in Technology across all the phases.

It has also established a series of working groups — as indicated in the organisation diagram .

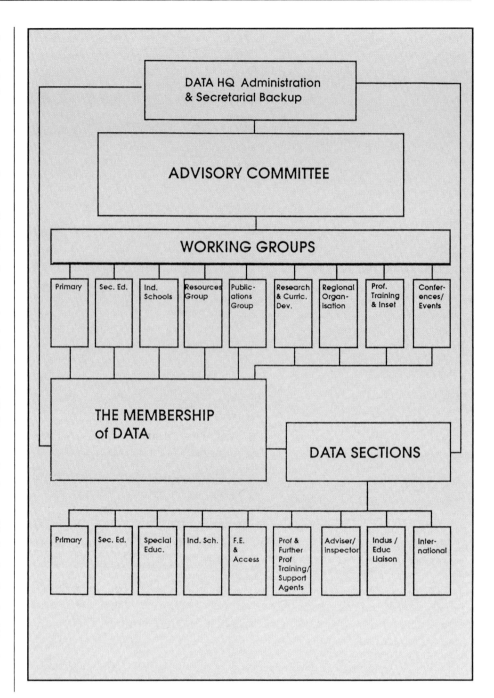

MEMBERSHIP CATEGORIES 1991

1 **Individual Membership**

    Great Britain £25

    Overseas £30

    Student £5

2 **Institutional Membership**

Primary schools (gps 1,2,3) and small preparatory schools £25

Primary schools (gp 4 and upwards) and preparatory schools £40

Secondary Schools (independent and maintained) £60

Departments in colleges of higher and further education, training institutions, polytechnics and universities £100

3. **Associate Membership**

For trading companies £200

4 **General Sponsors**

£1-2000

5 **Major Sponsors**

Of collaborative ventures and costed projects.

Subscription Form

Join NOW and get the remainder of 1990 FREE

DaTA

Smallpeice House
27 Newbold Terrace East
Leamington Spa
Warwickshire CV32 4ES
Telephone: 0926 315984
Fax: 0926 450679

THE DESIGN & TECHNOLOGY ASSOCIATION

APPLICATION FOR MEMBERSHIP 1991

Name _____ Dr Mr Mrs Miss Ms _____

Home address _____

_____

_____ Post code _____

Home Telephone Number _____

Institution Name & Address _____

_____

_____ Post code _____

Telephone Number _____ Extension _____

Please tick if you wish communications to be sent to your home ☐

or school/college ☐

Present Position including type of school, primary etc_____

_____

_____

Data sections to which you would like to be directly attached (please tick)	Area of present involvement (please tick):
☐ Primary	☐
☐ Secondary	☐
☐ Independent Schools	☐
☐ Further Education & Access	☐
☐ Professional & Further Professional Training/Support Agents	☐
☐ Adviser/Inspector	☐
☐ Industry/Education Liaison	☐
☐ International	☐

Please be sure to complete this application form and the appropriate part of the Subscription Form.

DaTA

Smallpeice House
27 Newbold Terrace East
Leamington Spa
Warwickshire CV32 4ES
Telephone: 0926 315984
Fax: 0926 450679

THE DESIGN & TECHNOLOGY ASSOCIATION

SUBSCRIPTION FORM FOR MEMBERSHIP 1991

Methods of Payment

Surname _____ Dr Mr Mrs Miss Ms

Forenames _____

1 Cheque

I enclose my cheque drawn on a United Kingdom Bank being my Member Subscription for 1991 (see below)   £ _____

(Membership £25/Student Membership £5)

or 2 Credit Card

Please charge my VISA/ACESS (delete as appropriate) card account with the amount shown, being the DATA Member Subscription for 1991 (see below).

Card No: ☐☐☐☐ ☐☐☐☐ ☐☐☐☐ ☐☐☐☐

Signature _____ Date_____ Expiry Date_____

Cardholder's Address _____   £ _____

_____ Post code_____

or 3 Credit Card Authority

I authorise Trentham Books, on behalf of DATA, until further notice in writing, to charge to my VISA/ACCESS (delete as appropriate) credit card account unspecified amounts in respect of my annual membership subscription.

Card No: ☐☐☐☐ ☐☐☐☐ ☐☐☐☐ ☐☐☐☐

Signature _____ Date_____ Expiry Date _____

Cardholder's address _____

_____ Post code _____

Please note that subscription payment by the above method (3) reduces our administration costs and saves you the bother of mailing an annual renewal slip.

ADDRESS (if not in box above)

_____

_____

Signature _____

Date _____

Member subscriptions for 1991 are set at £25. Student rate £5. (overseas £30 to include p&p.) Join NOW and get the remainder of 1990 FREE.

Design and Technology — Taking A Broad View

(An introduction to 'The Education (National Curriculum) (Attainment Target and Programmes of Study in Technology) Order 1990' Design and Technology and Information Technology

The new subject area; 'Technology', which includes Design and Technology and Information Technology, will be compulsory for all pupils from 5 to 16. What, essentially, is it? What is the justification for making it a compulsory part of the curriculum for every child; both those who will and those who will not become professional designers or technologists?

What is the underlying purpose and significance of 'Design and Technology', which defines the common cause to which colleagues with diverse skills, training and interests will contribute?

This introduction stands back from the detail of 'Attainment Targets' and 'Programmes of Study' to take a whole, and comprehensive, view of the idea of 'Design and Technology', not as a collection of separate subjects but as a single subject area with its own integrity and worth.

A striking feature of the National Curriculum document for Design and Technology is the absence, in it, of specified technological and factual content. Instead, it describes an activity concerned with developing pupils' capability, initiative and discernment in bringing about change in real circumstances. This, in turn, implies an approach to education designed to foster these personal skills as well as to encourage and enable the acquisition of knowledge.

Education itself is a similar kind of activity since it, too, involves taking deliberate action in order to influence conditions. Indeed the many complex personal skills and feelings involved in motivating and enabling learning: the interactive process we call education, may be regarded as a kind of 'Design and Technology' activity itself.

Because such activities are practised directly in real life they have special characteristics.

In real-life action the unexpected happens and it is impossible to predict, with certainly, the quality, effectiveness or total effect of its outcome. Real-Life activities carry an element of risk and absolute certainty is not possible however meticulous the planning. Even success and failure are matters of degree, and the means whereby we attempt to resolve the problems and opportunities we see and formulate, whether artefacts systems or environments, whilst they can be good, bad or indifferent, elegant, awkward, witty or pedestrian, can never be labelled 'right' or 'wrong' — except in a moral sense: and then only as a matter of opinion. There is no definitive answer at the back of a text book as there might be for a mathematical exercise.

Unlike such exercises the problems and opportunities of real life are not presented to us conveniently 'framed' within the confines of a hypothetical situation. They are not ready-made in the world outside oneself, waiting to be noticed. Human beings themselves, as individuals and in groups, conceive and formulate them.

To design is to arrive at an understanding of a situation in life, perhaps to conceive a problem or appreciate an opportunity: to envisage and take an initiative. In real life the urge to take action arises out of our interaction and involvement with people, things, events, ideas and materials. We make decisions about what should be done about them and how objectives might be realised. Ideas may well be nebulous: a mental imaging of vague possibilities. Questions arise: what do I wish to achieve? What means are available? How shall I set about meeting my purpose? What will it cost? How will I know whether I have succeeded? The thoughts do not follow a neat sequence as they must be written; mental images and notions evolve and are manipulated holistically. Together with observations, they coalesce and sequence has to be imposed at a later stage. Conceptions have to be outwardly reconstructed in words, sketches, models, diagrams or other external media for by doing so ideas are clarified to ourselves and rendered accessible to others. Action taken towards meeting the self-imposed 'problem': of 'externalising' ideas and intentions, is itself part of this search for a resolution. Attempting a resolution leads to greater awareness both of difficulties and opportunities. It can, and often does, lead to reassessment of the original issue.

Not only are real issues self-defined they are also self-assessed and, as we have seen, the routes we take towards their resolution are as complex as they are fascinating. The whole activity, not only an 'end product', is important educationally. Education is a complex of such activities, so is DIY, home management, time-tabling, architecture, fashion design, mechanical and electronic engineering and any other practical real-life activity.

Fun, humour, communication and expression are as likely to be justifiable, practical and worthy design purposes as any other. The same applies to aesthetic problems or opportunities. Moreover they are essential ingredients in any ambience calculated to encourage inventiveness.

Becoming involved in meeting a purpose which we have ourselves decided is worth our attention usually gives us a motivation we might not otherwise have and this is a powerful educational asset. Taking practical action in the world (as in educating children and students) is concerned to influence the future in some way, however slight — to bring about change.

Of educational importance, and crucial to design and technology activity, is the fact that bringing about change in the world also brings about change in oneself. It is a learn-

ing process. The degree of 'success' or 'failure' attained in a project is not to be equated directly 'with educational gain. 'Mistakes' and errors of judgement can be very instructive! This is why it is valuable for pupils to record and discuss their own progress and ideas. In this way insights may be gained into the thinking which has taken place.

We live and learn.

Although it will provide a sound and extremely useful foundation for professional training, Design and Technology Education from 5 to 16 is not intended to make every child a professional designer or technician any more than Mathematics and Science are intended as groundings only for future professionals in those fields. Just as we all make use of language mathematics, we all manipulate the environment and continually try to meet self-conceived problems and opportunities relating to it. We all make use of technology; employing, and sometimes creating, techniques and methods; proposing systems, recipes and procedures in order to meed our requirements.

In everyday life we are all designers. In their work, teachers, (amongst others) are designers

In their learning many children have not, in the past, had sufficient opportunity to exercise initiative, imagination and discrimination in meeting 'designerly problems' and in following up their own ideas.

Design/Technology/IT' seeks to repair this serious omission.

Though Design and Technology is a new subject area in its own right, it owes its genesis to some existing practice. In Art and Design, Business Studies, CDT and Home Economics where a practical 'problem-solving' approach has been adopted and in Primary Schools where 'learning through doing' has been practised, teachers will find the new ground not altogether unfamiliar.

Specialist teachers in the practical subject areas of secondary education will, in many cases, have to reorganise in order to work more closely

together. One kind of decision which will increasingly have to be made by pupils, guided by staff, is in their choice of media and techniques through which their proposals might best be realised. They will need to be able to select from, and make the fullest possible use of, the various sources of advice, guidance, expert knowledge, facilities and materials possible in their school, and even outside the school, wherever this can be arranged.

Both group and individual projects will be undertaken and even though projects will need to be negotiated with staff (a learning experience in itself!) the factual and technological learning consequent upon them is bound to be diverse. The learning environment of the child, of which the school is but a part, also influences this. So do the teachers and others who will make constructive comment and to whom the pupil will turn for advice and guidance. he or she will discover that different people have different and distinctive ideas about what is worth doing, what would be interesting to do and about how to set about doing it! There is a great deal to be learnt about people and how to communicate with them. Communication and perception, too, are necessary skills in finding out what people's needs are and in understanding and catering for them. Doctors, architects, interior designers and hairdressers do this. The assessment of need and the ability to create opportunities in the essence of research into market possibilities. personal and communication skills, together with estimation costs, time, and logistical planning, at however modest a level, involves imagination and flair: part of designerly activity; part of business and professional acumen and integrity.

It will be necessary to start pupils working in this way, especially where they have been used to having strict briefs given to them. Initiative is not developed or encouraged by removing the necessity to use it. Nor is it something which pupils can be expected suddenly to turn on after years of prescription! But projects often arise out of work already done and, with older pupils, class as well as individual study and discussion of interests and enterprises undertaken by themselves and others both inside and outside of school can be a starting point. The change of regime here will be most readily accepted by pupils where efforts are made to avoid identifying the subject area with any one of the subjects which will be initially involved and to make it clear that staff associated with them are now working as a team alongside the pupils. Indeed the involvement of the whole curriculum, hence to some degree the whole staff, though impractical for regular meetings, is nevertheless inevitable. Expression in language, mathematics, science and geography are examples. Written and verbal communication, calculation, the use of scientific principles, and understanding of the relationship of human beings animals and plants to habitat enter and relate to this subject area.

It will be important to develop a culture of involvement in which co-operation amongst pupils and staff is accepted as a congenial, necessary, and valuable part of life broadening out from the immediate context of family and school into the wider community and environment. Interest and the sharing of ideas amongst individuals engaged in their own project as well as collaboration amongst members of groups sharing and working towards common objectives, heightens the need and encourages the desire to communicate. Opportunities to do so through a variety of media offer exciting design challenges and possibilities in themselves.

The artefacts, systems and environments we create cannot exist in isolation. We inevitably design in a context and the quality and success, commercial or otherwise, of our creations must be judged as elements in that context: as contributors to it. The contexts of home and school: so-cieties in microcosm, point to the valuable contribution which those with home Economics expertise can make. Of the 'subjects' initially establishing Design/Technology at Secondary level, it is the only one whose base is contextual.

Because Design and Technology is an activity, capability in that activity is assessed. it involves the following elements, though it must be stressed the list is certainly not intended to suggest an order of activity or to imply that the elements are separate: they merge and interchange, consideration of each one can lead to modification of the others.

The capacity to...

decide, and give reasons for deciding, in collaboration with staff, upon an issue which might be addressed.
carry out research and enquiry, plan and reconcile conflicting constraints and interests.
decide on means whereby a plan might be carried out and put the idea into practice.
take into account possible effects upon other people and the environment as a whole.
judge the worthiness of the proposal general,
be self-critical and make objective self- assessments: taking into account the quality of the outcome in functional, economic, aesthetic and moral terms and the quality of the thought process leading to it, whether it be an artefact, system or environment.
learn from the experience, to record actions and processes by various means and to be able to discourse in an informed and rational way on their activities.

Real life action is inevitably accompanied by learning; learning of skills both intellectual and manual. Possibly the most exciting aspect of this particular part of the National Curriculum is its strong and convincing epistemological basis: it is a way of knowing and of learning. It is an area in which thinking, on the part of the child-designer, is encouraged and developed.

The personal qualities which Design and Technology seeks to nurture are of value in every walk of life, in and out of the workplace, and fundamental to professionalism. The important related issue: the need for team work and personal involvement amongst those employed in manufacturing industry, which is now being recognised as urgent, is even more important in our schools.

To return to the teachers. Their brief has always been 'to bring about change'. The kind of change which education will put into effect is important both to the learners and to the society they will play their part in continuing and constructing. A strong interactive element, with its moral and social constructive emphases and clear epistemological strength give this subject area vast potential for good. There is a sense in which humankind designs itself. Design and technology is about our use and manipulation of an environment we are at last realising needs looking after. Whilst its value to industry and trade is important and readily appreciated, the long term value of this curriculum area to our children as constructors and decision makers of the future, with all the environmental and life style questions that task is likely to raise, is hardly less important. They will need to be adaptable, long-sighted, considerate of others, sensitive to qualify in life and ingenious indeed!

Being involved in a designing activity, teachers themselves are engaged in what might be described as 'D/T-Learning'. Observing and becoming involved in their pupils' projects, they will occupy a unique research position; able to gain insights into human motivation: the way in which we learn and what prompts us to take action in the world.

Thinking about thinking!

David Buchan